A Mother's
Book of Poems

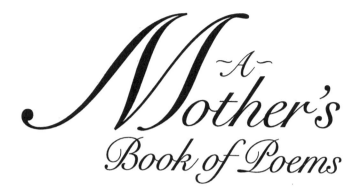

A Mother's Book of Poems

CB

CONTEMPORARY
BOOKS

CHICAGO

Library of Congress Cataloging-in-Publication Data

A mother's book of poems / compiled by Christine Benton.
      p.   cm.
   ISBN 0-8092-3525-0
    1. Mother and child—Poetry.   2. Motherhood—
Poetry.   3. Mothers— Poetry.   4. American poetry.
5. English poetry.   I. Benton, Christine.
PS595.M64M695   1994
811.008'03520431—dc20   94-29325
                                         CIP

This anthology was compiled by Christine M. Benton.

Published by Contemporary Books, Inc.
Two Prudential Plaza, Chicago, Illinois 60601-6790
Manufactured in the United States of America
International Standard Book Number: 0-8092-3525-0
10   9   8   7   6   5   4   3   2   1

The Baby

GEORGE MACDONALD
1824–1905

Where did you come from, baby dear?
Out of the everywhere into the here.

Where did you get your eyes so blue?
Out of the sky as I came through.

What makes the light in them sparkle and spin?
Some of the starry spikes left in.

Where did you get that little tear?
I found it waiting when I got here.

What makes your forehead so smooth and high?
A soft hand stroked it as I went by.

What makes your cheek like a warm white rose?
Something better than any one knows.

Whence that three-cornered smile of bliss?
Three angels gave me at once a kiss.

Where did you get that pearly ear?
God spoke, and it came out to hear.

Where did you get those arms and hands?
Love made itself into hooks and bands.

Feet, whence did you come, you darling things?
From the same box as the cherubs' wings.

How did they all just come to be you?
God thought about me, and so I grew.

But how did you come to us, you dear?
God thought of you, and so I am here.

Talisman

KATHARINE TYNAN HINKSON
1861–1931

All Heaven in my arm,
The child for a charm
'Gainst fear and 'gainst sorrow,
To-day and to-morrow.
The child for a charm
Betwixt me and harm.

O mouth, full of kisses!
Small body of blisses!
Your hand on my neck
And your cheek to my cheek.
What shall hurt me or harm
With all Heaven in my arm?

Birth

ANNIE R. STILLMAN
(GRACE RAYMOND)
1855–

Just when each bud was big with bloom,
   And as prophetic of perfume,
When spring, with her bright horoscope,
   Was sweet as an unuttered hope;

Just when the last star flickered out,
   And twilight, like a soul in doubt,
Hovered between the dark and dawn,
   And day lay waiting to be born;

Just when the gray and dewy air
   Grew sacred as an unvoiced prayer,
And somewhere through the dusk she heard
   The stirring of a nested bird,—

Four angels glorified the place:
   Wan Pain unveiled her awful face;
Joy, soaring, sang; Love, brooding, smiled;
   Peace laid upon her breast a child.

The Mother's Hope

LAMAN BLANCHARD
1803–1845

Is there, when the winds are singing
   In the happy summer-time,—
When the raptured air is ringing
With Earth's music heavenward springing,
   Forest chirp, and village chime,—
Is there, of the sounds that float
Unsighingly, a single note
Half so sweet and clear and wild
As the laughter of a child?

Listen! and be now delighted:
   Morn hath touched her golden strings;
Earth and Sky their vows have plighted;
Life and Light are reunited
   Amid countless carollings;
Yet, delicious as they are,
There's a sound that's sweeter far,—
One that makes the heart rejoice
More than all,—the human voice!

Organ finer, deeper, clearer,
   Though it be a stranger's tone,—
Than the winds or waters dearer,
More enchanting to the hearer,
   For it answereth to his own.
But, of all its witching words,
Sweeter than the song of birds,

Those are sweetest, bubbling wild
Through the laughter of a child.

Harmonies from time-touched towers,
   Haunted strains from rivulets,
Hum of bees among the flowers,
Rustling leaves, and silver showers,—
   These, erelong, the ear forgets;
But in mine there is a sound
Ringing on the whole year round,—
Heart-deep laughter that I heard
Ere my child could speak a word.

Ah! 't was heard by ear far purer,
   Fondlier formed to catch the strain,—
Ear of one whose love is surer,—
Hers, the mother, the endurer
   Of the deepest share of pain;
Hers the deepest bliss to treasure
Memories of that cry of pleasure,
Hers to hoard, a lifetime after,
Echoes of that infant laughter.

'T is a mother's large affection
   Hears with a mysterious sense,—
Breathings that evade detection,
Whisper faint, and fine inflection,
   Thrill in her with power intense.
Childhood's honeyed words untaught
Hiveth she in loving thought,—
Tones that never thence depart;
For she listens—with her heart.

To a Little Invisible Being Who Is Expected Soon to Become Visible

Anna Laetitia Barbauld
1743–1825

Germ of new life, whose powers expanding slow
For many a moon their full perfection wait—
Haste, precious pledge of happy love, to go
Auspicious borne through life's mysterious gate.

What powers lie folded in thy curious frame—
Senses from objects locked, and mind from thought!
How little canst thou guess thy lofty claim
To grasp at all the worlds the Almighty wrought!

And see, the genial season's warmth to share,
Fresh younglings shoot, and opening roses glow!
Swarms of new life exulting fill the air—
Haste, infant bud of being, haste to blow!

For thee the nurse prepares her lulling songs,
The eager matrons count the lingering days;
But far the most thy anxious parent longs
On thy soft cheek a mother's kiss to lay.

She only asks to lay her burden down,
That her glad arms that burden may resume;
And nature's sharpest pangs her wishes crown,
That free thee living from thy living tomb.

She longs to fold to her maternal breast
Part of herself, yet to herself unknown;
To see and to salute the stranger guest,
Fed with her life through many a tedious moon.

Come, reap thy rich inheritance of love!
Bask in the fondness of a Mother's eye!
Nor wit nor eloquence her heart shall move
Like the first accents of thy feeble cry.

Haste, little captive, burst thy prison doors!
Launch on the living world, and spring to light!
Nature for thee displays her various stores,
Opens her thousand inlets of delight.

If charmèd verse or muttered prayers had power
With favouring spells to speed thee on thy way,
Anxious I'd bid my beads each passing hour,
Till thy wished smile thy mother's pangs o'erpay.

To My Unborn Son

CAPTAIN CYRIL MORTON THORNE

"My son!" What simple, beautiful words!
   "My boy!" What a wonderful phrase!
We're counting the months till you come to us—
   The months, and the weeks, and the days!

"The new little stranger," some babes are called,
   But that's not what you're going to be;
With double my virtues and half of my faults,
   You can't be a stranger to me!

Your mother is straight as a sapling plant,
   The cleanest and best of her clan—
You're bone of her bone, and flesh of her flesh,
   And, by heaven, we'll make you a man!

Soon I shall take you in two strong arms—
   You that shall howl for joy—
With a simple, passionate, wonderful pride
   Because you are just—my boy!

And you shall lie in your mother's arms,
   And croon at your mother's breast,
And I shall thank God I am there to shield
   The two that I love the best.

A wonderful thing is a breaking wave,
    And sweet is the scent of spring,
But the silent voice of an unborn babe
    Is God's most beautiful thing.

We're listening now to that silent voice
    And waiting, your mother and I—
Waiting to welcome the fruit of our love
    When you come to us by and by.

We're hungry to show you a wonderful world
    With wonderful things to be done,
We're aching to give you the best of us both
    And we're lonely for you—my son!

The Poet and the Baby

PAUL LAURENCE DUNBAR
1872–1906

How's a man to write a sonnet, can you tell,—
How's he going to weave the dim, poetic spell,—
   When a-toddling on the floor
   Is the muse he must adore,
And this muse he loves, not wisely, but too well?

Now, to write a sonnet, every one allows,
One must always be as quiet as a mouse;
   But to write one seems to me
   Quite superfluous to be,
When you've got a little sonnet in the house.

Just a dainty little poem, true and fine,
That is full of love and life in every line,
   Earnest, delicate, and sweet,
   Altogether so complete
That I wonder what's the use of writing mine.

The Lamb

WILLIAM BLAKE
1757–1827

Little Lamb, who made thee?
Dost thou know who made thee?
Gave thee life & bid thee feed,
By the stream & o'er the mead;
Gave thee clothing of delight,
Softest clothing wooly bright;
Gave thee such a tender voice,
Making all the vales rejoice!
Little Lamb who made thee?
Dost thou know who made thee?

Little Lamb I'll tell thee,
Little Lamb I'll tell thee!
He is calléd by thy name,
For he calls himself a Lamb:
He is meek & he is mild,
He became a little child:
I a child & thou a lamb,
We are calléd by his name.
Little Lamb God bless thee.
Little Lamb God bless thee.

The New-Born Infant

CHARLES AND MARY LAMB
1775–1834 (CHARLES)
1764–1847 (MARY)

Whether beneath sweet beds of roses,
As foolish little Ann supposes,
The spirit of a babe reposes
  Before it to the body come;
Or, as philosophy more wise
Thinks, it descendeth from the skies,—
  We know the babe's now in the room,

And that is all which is quite clear
Even to philosophy, my dear.
  The God that made us can alone
Reveal from whence a spirit's brought
Into young life, to light, and thought;
  And this the wisest man must own.

We'll now talk of the babe's surprise,
When first he opens his new eyes,
  And first receives delicious food.
Before the age of six or seven,
To mortal children is not given
  Much reason; or I think he would

(And very naturally) wonder
What happy star he was born under,
    That he should be the only care
Of the dear sweet-food-giving lady,
Who fondly calls him her own baby,
    Her darling hope, her infant heir.

Lullaby

AKAN WOMAN; TRADITIONAL AFRICA

Someone would like to have you as her child
But you are mine.
Someone would like to rear you on a costly mat
But you are mine.
Someone would like to place you on a camel blanket
But you are mine.
I have you to rear on a torn old mat,
Someone would like to have you as her child
But you are mine.

The Children

CONSTANCE URDANG

1922–

What have I made
children
with voices like bull-calves bellowing
tall like the legendary children of the tribes
of the California
earth-children
to make friends with the burrowing moles
grass—
children sprouting everywhere (seeded
on impossible wings) wild
weed-children
          wood—
children
saplings all bark and twigs
air-children flying
children in the spring
where it bubbles up without let-up
slow sleepy children
heavy-lidded
nodding
in sun in shade
hot cold wet dry soft hard
tadpoles with see-through tails

naked nestlings
blind nurslings
sly

greedy
Oh, bite, teeth!
Kick, feet!
Pinch! Punch! (Pow!
Bam!! Blam!! Zap!!) AlL

          O

            V

              E

                R

made
love made
children

Alive

JUDITH WRIGHT
1915–

Light; and water. One drop.
Under the microscope
an outline. Slight
as a rim of glass;
barely and sparely there,
a scarcely-occupied shape.

What's more, the thing's alive.
How do I recognise
in a fleck so small
no human term applies—
no word's so minimal—
life's squirming throb and wave?

Locked in the focussed stare
of the lens, my sight
flinches: a tiny kick.
The life in me replies
signalling back
"You there: I here."
What matters isn't size.

What matters is . . . form. Form
concentrated, exact,
proof of a theorem

whose lines are lines of force
marking a limit. Trim,
somehow matter-of-fact,
even matter-of-course.
But alive. Like my eyes. Alive.

It's a Promise!

MARGARET FISHBACK
1904–1985

May heaven help me not to bore
    My friends with talk of teething.
They've met such miracles before,
    Including even breathing.

They've seen their share of babes in bed,
    Some somnolent, some sprightly.
They've heard what Little Mary said,
    And oh'd and ah'd politely.

So I'll be kind to kin and kith
    And mind my subject matter,
Unless they persecute me with
    Their own maternal chatter.

Two Temples

HATTIE VOSE HALL

A Builder builded a temple,
He wrought it with grace and skill;
Pillars and groins and arches
All fashioned to work his will.
Men said, as they saw its beauty,
"It shall never know decay;
Great is thy skill, O Builder!
Thy fame shall endure for aye."

A Mother builded a temple
With loving and infinite care,
Planning each arch with patience,
Laying each stone with prayer.
None praised her unceasing efforts,
None knew of her wondrous plan,
For the temple the Mother builded
Was unseen by the eyes of man.

Gone is the Builder's temple,
Crumpled into the dust;
Low lies each stately pillar,
Food for consuming rust.
But the temple the Mother builded
Will last while the ages roll,
For that beautiful unseen temple
Was a child's immortal soul.

Parental Recollections

CHARLES AND MARY LAMB
1775–1834 (CHARLES)
1764–1847 (MARY)

A child's a plaything for an hour;
   Its pretty tricks we try
For that or for a longer space;
   Then tire, and lay it by.

But I knew one, that to itself
   All seasons could control;
That would have mock'd the sense of pain
   Out of a grievëd soul.

Thou, straggler into loving arms,
   Young climber up of knees,
When I forget thy thousand ways,
   Then life and all shall cease.

Pregnancy

SANDRA McPHERSON
1943–

It is the best thing.
I should always like to be pregnant,

Tummy thickening like a yoghurt,
Unbelievable flower.

A queen is always pregnant with her country.
Sheba of questions

Or briny siren
At her difficult passage,

One is the mountain that moves
Toward the earliest gods.

Who started this?
An axis, a quake, a perimeter,

I have no decisions to master
That could change my frame

Or honor.
Immaculate. Or if it was not, perfect.

Pregnant, I'm highly explosive—
You can feel it, long before

Your seed will run back to hug you—
Squaring and cubing

Into reckless bones, bouncing odd ways
Like a football.

The heart sloshes through the microphone
Like falls in a box canyon.

The queen's only a figurehead.
Nine months pulled by nine

Planets, the moon slooping
Through its amnion sea,

Trapped, stone-mad . . . and three
Beings' lives gel in my womb.

Putting in the Seed

1874–1963

You come to fetch me from my work tonight
When supper's on the table, and we'll see
If I can leave off burying the white
Soft petals fallen from the apple tree
(Soft petals, yes, but not so barren quite,
Mingled with these, smooth bean and wrinkled pea;)
And go along with you ere you lose sight
Of what you came for and become like me,
Slave to a springtime passion for the earth.
How Love burns through the Putting in the Seed
On through the watching for that early birth
When, just as the soil tarnishes with weed,
The sturdy seedling with arched body comes
Shouldering its way and shedding the earth crumbs.

x

The Angels in the House

ANONYMOUS

Three pairs of dimpled arms, as white as snow,
  Held me in soft embrace;
Three little cheeks, like velvet peaches soft,
  Were placed against my face.

Three pairs of tiny eyes, so clear, so deep,
  Looked up in mine this even;
Three pairs of lips kissed me a sweet "Good-night,"
  Three little forms from Heaven.

Ah, it is well that "little ones" should love us;
  It lights our faith when dim,
To know that once our blesséd Saviour bade them
  Bring "little ones" to him.

And said he not, "Of such is Heaven," and blessed them,
  And held them to his breast?
Is it not sweet to know that, when they leave us,
  'Tis then they go to rest?

And yet, ye tiny angels of my house,
  Three hearts encased in mine,
How 'twould be shattered if the Lord should say,
  "Those angels are not thine!"

To a New Baby

STRICKLAND W. GILLILAN
1869–1954

Little kicking, cuddling thing,
You don't cry—you only sing!
Blinking eyes and stubby nose,
Mouth that mocks the budding rose,
Down for hair, peach-blows for hands—
Ah-h-h-h! Of all the "baby-grands"
Any one could wish to see,
You're the finest one for me!

Skin as soft as velvet is;
God (when you were only his)
Touched you on the cheek and chin—
Where he touched are dimples in.
Creases on your wrists, as though
Strings were fastened 'round them so
We could tie you tight and keep
You from leaving while we sleep.

Once I tried to look at you
From a stranger's point of view;
You were red and wrinkled; then
I just loved, and looked again;
What I saw was not the same;
In my eyes the blessed flame
Of a father's love consumed
Faults to strangers' eyes illumed.

Little squirming, cuddling thing!
Ere you shed each angel wing,
Did they tell you you were sent
With a cargo of content
To a home down here below
Where they hungered for you so?
Do you know, you flawless pearl,
How we love our baby girl?

All the Pretty Little Horses
TRADITIONAL USA

Hushaby
Don't you cry,
Go to sleep, little baby,
When you wake,
You shall have,
All the pretty little horses—
Blacks and bays,
Dapples and grays,
Coach and six-a little horses.
Hushaby,
Don't you cry,
Go to sleep, little baby.

Ma's Tools

ANONYMOUS

At home it seems to be the rule
Pa never has "the proper tool"
Or knack to fix things. For the stunt
That stumps ma, though, you'll have to hunt.

The caster on the table leg
Fell out. Pa said a wooden peg
Would fix it up. But ma kep' mum
An' fixed it with a wad of gum.

We could scarce open our front door,
It stuck so tight. An' pa, he swore
He'd "buy a plane" as big as life—
Ma fixed it with the carving knife.

The bureau drawer got stuck one day,
An', push or pull, 'twas there to stay.
Says pa, "Some day 'twill shrink, I hope."
Ma fixed it with a piece of soap.

The window-shade got out of whack,
'Twould not pull down, nor yet roll back.
Pa says, "No one can fix that thing."
Ma fixed it with a piece of string.

I broke the stove-door hinge one day.
('Twas cracked before, though, anyway.)
Pa said we'd put a new door in.
Ma grabbed her hair an' got a pin.

The bathtub drain got all clogged up.
Pa bailed the tub out with a cup—
He had a dreadful helpless look.
Ma cleaned it with a crochet-hook.

One day our old clock wouldn't start.
Pa said he'd take it all apart
Some day an' fix the ol' machine.
Ma soused the works in gasoline.

The garden-gate latch broke one day,
Cows ate our sweet corn up. An', say,
Pa scolded like a house afire
Ma fixed the latch up with hay wire.

So when my things gets out of fix
Do I ask pa to mend 'em? Nix!
But ma just grabs what's near at hand
An' togs things up to beat the band.

Baby Feet

Edgar A. Guest
1881–1959

Tell me, what is half so sweet
As a baby's tiny feet,
Pink and dainty as can be,
Like a coral from the sea?
Talk of jewels strung in rows,
Gaze upon those little toes,
Fairer than a diadem,
With the mother kissing them!

It is morning and she lies
Uttering her happy cries,
While her little hands reach out
For the feet that fly about.
Then I go to her and blow
Laughter out of every toe;
Hold her high and let her place
Tiny footprints on my face.

Little feet that do not know
Where the winding roadways go,
Little feet that never tire,
Feel the stones or trudge the mire,
Still too pink and still too small
To do anything but crawl,
Thinking all their wanderings fair,
Filled with wonders everywhere.

Little feet, so rich with charm,
May you never come to harm.
As I bend and proudly blow
Laughter out of every toe,
This I pray, that God above
Shall protect you with His love,
And shall guide those little feet
Safely down life's broader street.

Rocking My Child

GABRIELA MISTRAL
1889–1957

The sea its millions of waves
 is rocking, divine,
hearing the loving seas,
 I'm rocking my child.

The wandering wind in the night
 is rocking the fields of wheat,
hearing the loving winds,
 I'm rocking my child.

God the father his thousands of worlds
 is rocking without a sound.
Feeling his hand in the shadows,
 I'm rocking my child.

Translated by Perry Higman

The Household Sovereign

From *The Hanging of the Crane*

HENRY WADSWORTH LONGFELLOW
1807–1882

Seated I see the two again,
but not alone; they entertain
A little angel unaware,
With face as round as is the moon;
A royal guest with flaxen hair,
Who, throned upon his lofty chair,
Drums on the table with his spoon,
Then drops it careless on the floor,
To grasp at things unseen before.
Are these celestial manners? these
The ways that win, the arts that please?
Ah, yes; consider well the guest,
And whatsoe'er he does seems best;
He ruleth by the right divine
Of helplessness, so lately born
In purple chambers of the morn,
As sovereign over thee and thine.
He speaketh not, and yet there lies
A conversation in his eyes;
The golden silence of the Greek,
The gravest wisdom of the wise,
Not spoken in language, but in looks
More legible than printed books,
As if he could but would not speak.

And now, O monarch absolute,
Thy power is put to proof; for lo!
Resistless, fathomless, and slow,
The nurse comes rustling like the sea,
And pushes back thy chair and thee,
And so good night to King Canute.

The Anatomy of Melancholy

MARGARET FISHBACK
1904–1985

A little baby, when she cries,
Is a spectacular surprise.

Assorted lines distort her face,
And of her eyes there's not a trace.

Her infant nose has vanished, too,
And left a button for a clue.

But most mysterious of all,
Her rosebud mouth, which was so small,

Has suddenly become, instead,
A good deal bigger than her head.

My Little Girl

SAMUEL MINTURN PECK
1854–

My little girl is nested
　　Within her tiny bed,
With amber ringlets crested
　　Around her dainty head;
She lies so calm and stilly,
　　She breathes so soft and low,
She calls to mind a lily
　　Half-hidden in the snow.

A weary little mortal
　　Has gone to slumberland;
The Pixies at the portal
　　Have caught her by the hand.
She dreams her broken dolly
　　Will soon be mended there,
That looks so melancholy
　　Upon the rocking-chair.

I kiss your wayward tresses,
　　My drowsy little queen;
I know you have caresses
　　From floating forms unseen.

O, Angels, let me keep her
　　To kiss away my cares,
This darling little sleeper,
　　Who has my love and prayers!

32

Japanese Lullaby

EUGENE FIELD
1850–1895

Sleep, little pigeon, and fold your wings,—
   Little blue pigeon with velvet eyes;
Sleep to the singing of mother-bird swinging—
   Swinging the nest where her little one lies.

Away out yonder I see a star,—
   Silvery star with a tinkling song;
To the soft dew falling I hear it calling—
   Calling and tinkling the night along.

In through the window a moonbeam comes,—
   Little god moonbeam with misty wings;
All silently creeping, it asks: "Is he sleeping—
   Sleeping and dreaming while mother sings?"

Up from the sea there floats a sob
   Of the waves that are breaking upon the shore,
As though they were groaning in anguish, and
     moaning—
   Bemoaning the ship that shall come no more.

But sleep, little pigeon, and fold your wings,—
   Little blue pigeon with mournful eyes;
Am I not singing?—see, I am swinging—
   Swinging the nest where my darling lies.

On Viewing Her Sleeping Infant
(C[harles] C[owpe]r)

Written at the Park, Hertfordshire, in 1767

MARIA FRANCES CECILIA COWPER
1726–1797

I have seen the rosebud blow,
And in the jocund sumbeam glow,
Sportive lambs on airy mound,
Skipping o'er the velvet ground;
And the sprightly-footed morn,
When every hedge and every thorn
Was decked in spring's apparel gay,
All the pride of opening May:
Yet—nor rosebud early blowing,
In the jocund sunbeam glowing,
Nor the sportive lambs that bound
O'er the sweet enamelled ground,
Nor the sprightly-footed morn,
When brilliants hang on every thorn—
These not half thy charms display:
Thou art fairer still than they,
Still more innocent, more gay!

  Mild thou art as evening showers,
Stealing on ambrosial flowers;
Or the silver-shining moon
Riding near her highest noon.
Who, to view thy peaceful form,
Heeds the winter-blowing storm?
Thy smiles the calm of heaven bestow,

And soothe the bitterest sense of woe!
As bees, that suck the honeyed store
From silvery dews, on blushing flower,
So on thy cheek's more lovely bloom
I scent the rose's quick perfume.
Thine ivory extended arms,
To hold the heart—what powerful charms!
   Come, soft babe! with every grace
Glowing in thy matchless face—
Come, unconscious innocence!
Every winning charm dispense—
All thy little arts—thine own—
For thou the world hast never known!
And yet thou canst, a thousand ways,
A mother's partial fondness raise!
And all her anxious soul detain
With many a link of pleasing chain;
Leading captive at thy will,
Following thy little fancies still.
Though nature yet thy tongue restrains,
Nor canst thou lisp thy joys or pains!
Yet every gracious meaning lies
Within the covert of thine eyes:
Wit, and the early dawn of sense,
Live in their silent eloquence.
   May every future day impart
New virtues to adorn thy heart;
May gracious heaven profusely shed
Its choicest blessings o'er thy head!
Blessed, and a blessing, mayst thou prove,
Till crowned with endless joys above!

Baby's Favorite Resort

STRICKLAND W. GILLILAN
1869–1954

They talk of sea-shore havens and the mountain-top
    hotels;
They prate of quiet country lanes where peace in plenty
    dwells;
They speak of winter-comfort in the Southland and the
    West—
The hollow of my mother's arms I'm mighty sure's the
    best.

They sing of lakeside places where 'tis cool in
    summertime;
They boast of restful harbors in some distant foreign
    clime;
They seek the falls in springtime and the springs in early
    fall—
I know a spot on mother's arm that is the best of all.

The journey thither costs me but a fretful cry or two;
The time it takes is nothing—in a trice the trip is
    through.
The service there is perfect and the food is quite the
    best—
I know no place that's finer than my mother's arm, for
    rest.

Little Son

GEORGIA DOUGLAS JOHNSON
1886–1966

The very acme of my woe,
  The pivot of my pride,
My consolation, and my hope
  Deferred, but not denied.
The substance of my every dream,
  The riddle of my plight,
The very world epitomized
  In turmoil and delight.

Fantasia

EVE MERRIAM
1916–

I dream
of
giving birth
to
a child
who will ask
'Mother,
what was war?'

Thoughts About My Daughter Before Sleep

SANDRA HOCHMAN
1936–

1

Ariel, one true
Miracle of my life, my golden
Sparrow, burning in your crib
As the rain falls over the meadow
And the squirrel corn,
While the fragrant hyacinth
Sleeps in its bed in the rich
Mud of the north, while foamflowers
Climb through small arches of rain, and the sun
Brings lilies and dark blue berries
In cluster, leaf on leaf again,
I wonder how I came to give you life.

2

Here, where the twisted stalks
Of deer grass zigzag
Branches from the tree, where
Honeysuckles trumpet, "All joy
Is in the dark vessels of the skin!"
And thorn apples open their leaves,
I marvel to have made you perfect
As a small plant, you, filled
Up with sunlight and
Fragrant as ferns.

3

And before snow
Covers ivy and bluet
Shall I teach you this old
Summer's lesson
About seeds? About miracles
Of growth? Here are the bursting zinnias,
Asters, prongs
Of phlox—shall I wake you?
Take you out of sleep
And roll you in the apple fields?

4

And through you
I am born as I lie down
In the seedbox of my own beginnings,
Opening the wild part of me,
Once lost once lost
As I was breathing
In the vines of childhood.

Little Feet

ELIZABETH AKERS
1832–

Two little feet, so small that both may nestle
  In one caressing hand,—
Two tender feet upon the untried border
  Of life's mysterious land.

Dimpled, and soft, and pink as peach-tree blossoms,
  In April's fragrant days,
How can they walk among the briery tangles,
  Edging the world's rough ways?

These rose-white feet, along the doubtful future,
  Must bear a mother's load;
Alas! since Woman has the heaviest burden,
  And walks the harder road.

Love, for a while, will make the path before them
  All dainty, smooth, and fair,—
Will cull away the brambles, letting only
  The roses blossom there.

But when the mother's watchful eyes are shrouded
  Away from sight of men,
And these dear feet are left without her guiding,
  Who shall direct them then?

How will they be allured, betrayed, deluded,
  Poor little untaught feet!

Into what dreary mazes will they wander,
 What dangers will they meet?

Will they go stumbling blindly in the darkness
 Of Sorrow's tearful shades?
Or find the upland slopes of Peace and Beauty,
 Whose sunlight never fades?

Will they go toiling up Ambition's summit,
 The common world above?
Or in some nameless vale, securely sheltered,
 Walk side by side with Love?

Some feet there be which walk Life's track unwounded,
 Which find but pleasant ways:
Some hearts there be to which this life is only
 A round of happy days.

But these are few. Far more there are who wander
 Without a hope or friend,—
Who find their journey full of pains and losses,
 And long to reach the end.

How shall it be with her, the tender stranger,
 Fair-faced and gentle-eyed,
Before whose unstained feet the world's rude highway
 Stretches so fair and wide?

Ah! who may read the future? For our darling
 We crave all blessings sweet,
And pray that He who feeds the crying ravens
 Will guide the baby's feet.

Any Mother

KATHARINE TYNAN HINKSON
1861–1931

There is no height, no depth, my own, could set us apart,
Body of mine and soul of mine: heart of my heart!

There is no sea so deep, my own, no mountain so high,
That I should not come to you if I heard you cry.

There is no Hell so sunken, no Heaven so steep,
Where I should not seek my own, find you and keep.

Now you are round and soft to see, sweet as a rose,
Not a stain on my spotless one, white as the snows.

If some day you came to me heavy with sin,
I, your mother, would run to the door and let you in.

I would wash you white again with my tears and grief,
Body of mine and soul of mine, till you found relief.

Though you had sinned all sins there are 'twixt east and
    west,
You should find my arms wide for you, your head on my
    breast.

Child, if I were in Heaven one day and you were in
    Hell—
Angels white as my spotless one stumbled and fell—

I would leave for you the fields of God and Queen
  Mary's feet,
Straight to the heart of Hell would go, seeking my sweet.

God mayhap would turn Him around at sound of the
  door:
Who is it goes out from Me to come back no more?

Then the blessed Mother of God would say from her
  throne:
Son, 'tis a mother goes to Hell, seeking her own.

Body of mine, and Soul of mine, born of me,
Thou who wert once little Jesus beside my knee,

It is like to that all mothers are made: Thou madest them
  so.
Body of mine and Soul of mine, do I not know?

The Dirty-Billed Freeze Footy

Judith Hemschemeyer
1935–

Remember that Saturday morning
Mother forgot the word gull?

We were all awake but still in bed
and she called out, "Hey kids!

What's the name of that bird that eats garbage
and stands around in cold water on the beach?"

And you, the quick one, the youngest daughter
piped right back: "A dirty-billed freeze footy!"

And she laughed till she was weak,
until it hurt her. And you had done it:

reduced our queen to warm and helpless rubble.

And the rest of the day, baking or cleaning
or washing our hair until it squeaked,

whenever she caught sight of you
it would start all over again.

What Are Little Boys Made Of?

ANONYMOUS

What are little boys made of, made of?
What are little boys made of?
  Frogs and snails
  And puppy-dogs' tails,
That's what little boys are made of.

What are little girls made of, made of?
What are little girls made of?
  Sugar and spice
  And all things nice,
That's what little girls are made of.

Monday's Child Is Fair of Face

ANONYMOUS

Monday's child is fair of face,
Tuesday's child is full of grace,
Wednesday's child is full of woe,
Thursday's child has far to go,
Friday's child is loving and giving,
Saturday's child works hard for a living,
And the child that is born on the Sabbath day
Is bonny and blithe, and good and gay.

Boy or Girl?

EDGAR A. GUEST

1881–1959

Some folks pray for a boy, and some
For a golden-haired little girl to come.
　Some claim to think there is more of joy
　Wrapped up in the smile of a little boy,
　While others pretend that the silky curls
　And plump, pink cheeks of the little girls
　Bring more of bliss to the old home place
　Than a small boy's queer little freckled face.

Now which is better, I couldn't say
If the Lord should ask me to choose to-day;
　If He should put in a call for me
　And say: "Now what shall your order be,
　A boy or girl? I have both in store—
　Which of the two are you waiting for?"
　I'd say with one of my broadest grins:
　"Send either one, if it can't be twins."

I've heard it said, to some people's shame,
They cried with grief when a small boy came,
　For they wanted a girl. And some folks I know
　Who wanted a boy, just took on so
　When a girl was sent. But it seems to me
　That mothers and fathers should happy be
　To think, when the Stork has come and gone,
　That the Lord would trust them with either one.

Boy or girl? There can be no choice;
There's something lovely in either voice.
  And all that I ask of the Lord to do
  Is to see that the mother comes safely through.
  And guard the baby and have it well,
  With a perfect form and a healthy yell,
  And a pair of eyes and a shock of hair
  Then, boy or girl—and its dad won't care.

Hush-a-ba, Burdie

ANONYMOUS

Hush-a-ba, burdie, croon, croon,
  Hush-a-ba, burdie, croon.
The sheep are gane tae the siller wid,
  An the coos are gane tae the broom, broom.

An it's braw milkin the kye, kye,
  It's braw milkin the kye,
The birds are singin, the bells are ringin,
  And the wild deer come gallopin by.

Hush-a-ba, burdie, croon, croon,
  Hush-a-ba, burdie, croon,
The gaits are gane tae the mountain hie,
  An they'll no be hame till noon.

For My Son

MURIEL RUKEYSER
1913–1980

You come from poets, kings, bankrupts, preachers,
    attempted bankrupts, builders of cities, salesmen,
the great rabbis, the kings of Ireland, failed drygoods
    storekeepers, beautiful women of the songs,
great horsemen, tyrannical fathers at the shore of
      ocean,
    the western mothers looking west beyond from
        their windows,
the families escaping over the sea hurriedly and by
      night—
the roundtowers of the Celtic violet sunset,
the diseased, the radiant, fliers, men thrown out of
      town,
    the man bribed by his cousins to stay out of
        town,
      teachers, the cantor on Friday evening, the lurid
        newspapers,
strong women gracefully holding relationship, the
      Jewish
    girl going to parochial school, the boys racing
        their iceboats on the Lakes,
the woman still before the diamond in the velvet
      window,
    saying "Wonder of nature."

Like all men,
you come from singers, the ghettoes, the famines,
    wars and
  refusal of wars, men who built villages
that grew to our solar cities, students, revolutionists,
    the
  pouring of buildings, the market newspapers,
a poor tailor in a darkening room,
a wilderness man, the hero of mines, the
        astronomer, a
  white-faced woman hour on hour teaching piano
        and her crippled wrist,
like all men,
you have not seen your father's face
but he is known to you forever in song, the coast of
    the
  skies, in dream, wherever you find man playing
        his
    part as father, father among our light, among
        our darkness,
and in your self made whole, whole with yourself
    and
  whole with others,
the stars your ancestors.

The Baby

MARY RAYMOND SHIPMAN ANDREWS
-1936

I am The Baby,
I own this room and everything
   that's in sight—
I own the pink blankets and all the
   pillows and this brass crib that's
   so shiny and bright.
I'd like to suck the crib, but I can't,
   because it doesn't come close to
   my mouth
Like bottles and woolly blankets,
   anyhow it's mine, east to west and
   north to south.
That couple of old persons around
   20 who refer to themselves as
   "father" and "mother"—
They're mine too, and when I'm engaged
   with important thoughts
   they're a bother—
Yet there's a dreamy satisfaction in
   owning them, and in seeing them
   make fools of themselves to amuse me.
The Person in Skirts assures me
   often that nobody shall abuse me
Because I'm her owny-wowny lamby-petty—
   I wonder why she thinks that sort of
   asininity

Is appropriate to me, fresh from the stars
   and the whirl of infinity?
I fix her with a cold stare, but she
   only says: "Look, Teddy—
He acts as if he knew us, and owned us
   and scorned us already."
Yet I'm getting used to their queer games
   and they begin to appeal to me.
It seems it's they who soak me in
   pink blankets and adoration and
   every day deal to me
Through my nurse and my minions
   in general the sundry warm bottles
   and such.
Which are the real facts of the universe
   and please me very much.
The Person in Trousers one day was
   left alone with me
And I stared up and he stared down,
   frowning hard, as if he'd pick a
   bone with me.
So after a while I remarked: "Bh"
   and he laughed and he said: "You
   little cuss,
Suppose we seize this chance for an
   interview, just us"
And he bent over my crib and to my
   astonishment lifted me,
Though I knew that, after he'd once
   gripped, not for worlds would he
   have shifted me.

51

But he got me up safe in his huge
   claws, and held me, and, you know,
   it was nice,
Though his hands were so gentle and
   terrified, they were comfy and strong
   as a vise;
Then he looked at me, very much as
   The Person in Skirts looks, which
   I didn't know he knew how,
And he whispered straight at me,
   "Little cuss, there's going to be
   one horrid big row
If you don't get all that's coming to
   you, love and care and food and
   chances.
If you don't, it's your father will
   know the reason why, and such are
   the circumstances."
Then he laid me down, as if I were
   trinitrotoluol at least.
And I googled up at him, and
   laughed much like a fish at a
   feast
And since then I like him to come,
   and to touch me, and I rather
Am inclined to consider it's a good
   asset to have a father.

If You'll Only Go to Sleep

GABRIELA MISTRAL
1889–1957

The crimson rose
plucked yesterday,
the fire and cinnamon
of the carnation,

the bread I baked
with anise seed and honey,
and the goldfish
flaming in its bowl.

All these are yours,
baby born of woman,
if you'll only
go to sleep.

A rose, I say!
And a carnation!
Fruit, I say!
And honey!

And a sequined goldfish,
and still more I'll give you
if you'll only sleep
till morning.

Translated by Doris Dana

To a Child Who Inquires

OLGA PETROVA

1886–1977

How did you come to me, my sweet?
  From the land that no man knows?
Did Mr. Stork bring you here on his wings?
  Were you born in the heart of a rose?

Did an angel fly with you down from the sky?
  Were you found in a gooseberry patch?
Did a fairy bring you from fairyland
  To my door—that was left on a latch?

No—my darling was born of a wonderful love,
  A love that was Daddy's and mine.
A love that was human, but deep and profound,
  A love that was almost divine.

Do you remember, sweetheart, when we went to the zoo,
  And we saw the big bear with a grouch?
And the tigers and lions, and that tall kangaroo
  That carried her babe in a pouch?

Do you remember I told you she kept them there safe
  From the cold and the wind, till they grew
Big enough to take care of themselves? And, dear heart,
  That's just how I first cared for you.

I carried you under my heart, my sweet,
  And I sheltered you safe from alarms;
Then one wonderful day the dear God looked down,
  And I snuggled you tight in my arms.

Boyhood

WASHINGTON ALLSTON
1779–1843

Ah, then how sweetly closed those crowded days!
The minutes parting one by one, like rays
  That fade upon a summer's eve.
But O, what charm or magic numbers
Can give me back the gentle slumbers
  Those weary, happy days did leave?
When by my bed I saw my mother kneel,
  And with her blessing took her nightly kiss;
  Whatever time destroys, he cannot this;—
E'en now that nameless kiss I feel.

Nice Baby

JUDITH VIORST
1931–

Last year I talked about black humor and the impact of
   the common market on the European economy and
Threw clever little cocktail parties in our discerningly
   eclectic living room
With the Spanish rug and the hand-carved Chinese chest
   and the lucite chairs and
Was occasionally hungered after by highly placed men in
   communications, but
This year we have a nice baby
And Pablum drying on our Spanish rug,
And I talk about nursing versus sterilization
While the men in communications
Hunger elsewhere.

Last year I studied flamenco and had my ears pierced
   and
Served an authentic fondue on the Belgian marble table
   of our discerningly eclectic dining area, but
This year we have a nice baby
And Spock on the second shelf of our Chinese chest,
And instead of finding myself I am doing my best
To find a sitter
For the nice baby banging the Belgian marble with his
   cup
While I heat the oven up
For the TV dinners.

Last year I had a shampoo and set every week and
Slept an unbroken sleep beneath the Venetian chandelier
   of our discerningly eclectic bedroom, but
This year we have a nice baby,
And Gerber's strained bananas in my hair,
And gleaming beneath the Venetian chandelier,
A diaper pail, a Portacrib, and him,
A nice baby, drooling on our antique satin spread
While I smile and say how nice. It is often said
That motherhood is very maturing.

Which Shall It Be?

ETHEL LYNN BEERS

1827–1879

"Which shall it be? Which shall it be?"
I look'd at John—John look'd at me
(Dear, patient John, who loves me yet
As well as though my locks were jet);
And when I found that I must speak,
My voice seem'd strangely low and weak;
"Tell me again what Robert said."
And then I, listening, bent my head.
"This is his letter: 'I will give
A house and land while you shall live,
If, in return, from out your seven,
One child to me for aye is given.' "
I look'd at John's old garments worn,
I thought of all that John had borne
Of poverty and work and care,
Which I, though willing, could not share;
I thought of seven mouths to feed,
Of seven little children's need,
And then of this. "Come, John," said I,
"We'll choose among them as they lie
Asleep;" so, walking hand in hand,
Dear John and I survey'd our band.
First to the cradle lightly stepp'd,
Where the new nameless baby slept.
"Shall it be Baby?" whispered John.

I took his hand, and hurried on
To Lily's crib. Her sleeping grasp
Held her old doll within its clasp;
Her dark curls lay like gold alight,
A glory 'gainst the pillow white.
Softly her father stoop'd to lay
His rough hand down in loving way,
When dream or whisper made her stir,
Then huskily said John, "Not her, not her!"
We stopp'd beside the trundle bed,
And one long ray of lamplight shed
Athwart the boyish faces there,
In sleep so pitiful and fair;
I saw on Jamie's rough, red cheek
A tear undried. Ere John could speak,
"He's but a baby, too," said I,
And kiss'd him as we hurried by.
Pale, patient Robbie's angel face
Still in his sleep bore suffering's trace.
"No, for a thousand crowns, not him!"
We whisper'd, while our eyes were dim.
Poor Dick! bad Dick! our wayward son,
Turbulent, reckless, idle one—
Could he be spared? Nay; He who gave
Bids us befriend him to his grave;
Only a mother's heart can be
Patient enough for such as he;
"And so," said John, "I would not dare
To send him from her bedside prayer."

Then stole we softly up above
And knelt by Mary, child of love.
"Perhaps for her 'twould better be,"
I said to John. Quite silently
He lifted up a curl astray
Across her cheek in wilful way,
And shook his head: "Nay, love; not thee,"
The while my heart beat audibly.
Only one more, our eldest lad,
Trusty and truthful, good and glad—
So like his father. "No, John, no—
I cannot, will not, let him go."
And so we wrote, in courteous way,
We could not give one child away;
And afterward toil lighter seem'd,
Thinking of that which we dream'd,
Happy in truth that not one face
We miss'd from its accustom'd place;
Thankful to work for all the seven,
Trusting the rest to One in heaven.

Poem to Ease Birth

ANONYMOUS; NAHUATL (AZTEC)

in the house with the tortoise chair
   she will give birth to the pearl
              to the beautiful feather

in the house of the goddess who sits on a tortoise
   she will give birth to the necklace of pearls
              to the beautiful feathers we are

there she sits on the tortoise
   swelling to give us birth

on your way on your way
   child be on your way to me here
           you whom I made new

come here child   come be pearl
           be beautiful feather

Translated by Anselm Hollo

Close to Me

GABRIELA MISTRAL
1889–1957

Little fleece of my flesh
that I wove in my womb,
little shivering fleece,
sleep close to me!

The partridge sleeps in the clover
hearing its heart beat.
My breathing will not wake you.
Sleep close to me!

Little trembling blade of grass
astonished to be alive,
don't leave my breast.
Sleep close to me!

I who have lost everything
am now afraid to sleep.
Don't slip away from my arms.
Sleep close to me!

Translated by Doris Dana

Alice Ray

SARAH JOSEPHA HALE
1788–1879

The birds their love-notes warble
　　Among the blossomed trees;
The flowers are sighing forth their sweets
　　To wooing honey-bees;
The glad brook o'er a pebbly floor
　　Goes dancing on its way,—
But not a thing is so like spring
　　As happy Alice Ray.

An only child was Alice,
　　And, like the blest above,
The gentle maid had ever breathed
　　An atmosphere of love;
Her father's smile like sunshine came,
　　Like dew her mother's kiss;
Their love and goodness made her home,
　　Like heaven, the place of bliss.

Beneath such tender training,
　　The joyous child had sprung,
Like one bright flower, in wild-wood bower,
　　And gladness round her flung;
And all who met her blessed her,
　　And turned again to pray
That grief and care might ever spare
　　The happy Alice Ray.

The gift that made her charming
   Was not from Venus caught;
Nor was it, Pallas-like, derived
   From majesty of thought;
Her heathful cheek was tinged with brown,
   Her hair without a curl—
But then her eyes were love-lit stars,
   Her teeth as pure as pearl.

And when in merry laughter
   Her sweet, clear voice was heard,
It welled from out her happy heart
   Like carol of a bird;
And all who heard were moved to smiles,
   As at some mirthful lay,
And to the stranger's look replied,
   " 'T is that dear Alice Ray."

And so she came, like sunbeams
   That bring the April green;
As type of nature's royalty,
   They called her "Woodburn's queen!"
A sweet, heart-lifting cheerfulness,
   Like spring-time of the year,
Seemed ever on her steps to wait,—
   No wonder she was dear.

Her world was ever joyous—
  She thought of grief and pain
As giants in the olden time,
  That ne'er would come again;
The seasons all had charms for her,
  She welcomed each with joy,—
The charm that in her spirit lived
  No changes could destroy.

Her heart was like a fountain,
  The waters always sweet,—
Her pony in the pasture,
  The kitten at her feet,
The ruffling bird of Juno, and
  The wren in the old wall,
Each knew her loving carefulness,
  And came at her soft call.

Her love made all things lovely,
  For in the heart must live
The feeling that imparts the charm,—
  We gain by what we give.

Love at First Sight

MARGARET FISHBACK
1904–1985

Dear Valentine, for you I sigh—
When first we met, you took my eye.

And now I love you even more
Than I have loved you heretofore.

Here is my heart. I beg you, take it,
Though you will barge ahead, and break it.

Don't hesitate, for I'll contrive
To smile assurance, and survive.

And you will have such shameless fun
When you consume it, little son.

I, too, can see that it's enticing—
It's made of gingerbread with icing.

Laus Infantium

WILLIAM CANTON
1845–1926

In praise of little children I will say
God first made man, then found a better way
For woman, but his third way was the best.
Of all created things, the loveliest
And most divine are children. Nothing here
Can be to us more gracious or more dear.
And though, when God saw all his works were good,
There was no rosy flower of babyhood,
'T was said of children in a later day
That none could enter Heaven save such as they.

The earth, which feels the flowering of a thorn,
Was glad, O little child, when you were born;
The earth, which thrills when skylarks scale the blue,
Soared up itself to God's own Heaven in you;

And Heaven, which loves to lean down and to glass
Its beauty in each dewdrop on the grass,—
Heaven laughed to find your face so pure and fair,
And left, O little child, its reflex there.

Weighing the Baby

ETHEL LYNN BEERS

1827–1879

"How many pounds does the baby weigh—
  Baby who came but a month ago?
How many pounds from the crowning curl
  To the rosy point of the restless toe?"

Grandfather ties the 'kerchief knot,
  Tenderly guides the swinging weight,
And carefully over his glasses peers
  To read the record, "Only eight."

Softly the echo goes around:
  The father laughs at the tiny girl;
The fair young mother sings the words,
  While grandmother smooths the golden curl.

And stooping above the precious thing,
  Nestles a kiss within a prayer,
Murmuring softly "Little one,
  Grandfather did not weigh you fair."

Nobody weighed the baby's smile,
  Or the love that came with the helpless one;
Nobody weighed the threads of care,
  From which a woman's life is spun.

No index tells the mighty worth
    Of a little baby's quiet breath—
A soft, unceasing metronome,
    Patient and faithful until death.

Nobody weighed the baby's soul,
    For here on earth no weights there be
That could avail; God only knows
    Its value in eternity.

Only eight pounds to hold a soul
    That seeks no angel's silver wing,
But shrines it in this human guise,
    Within so frail and small a thing!

Oh, mother! laugh your merry note,
    Be gay and glad, but don't forget
From baby's eyes looks out a soul
    That claims a home in Eden yet.

Live for it

ELLEN BASS
1947–

Window curtain nodding in the May breeze
birds outside singing their high sweet scatter
inside a fly frantic against its mistake, buzzing the
    walls, the glass,
    small thuds of failure—

Since my daughter's birth five rich years ago, I have
    never been without
    the mantle of nuclear holocaust.
I feel it like crepe against my cheek.

The first year, I wept.
The exhaustion of nighttime nursing,
the demand of infant need,
the tidal love that broke upon my abundant body
    left me sensible to knowledge I had shielded
        from so deftly before.

She reads now, prints, bounces a ball, ties bows,
    washes her feet in the bath.
She says, "If you read one more story,
    I'll let you sleep as late as you want in the
        morning."
She says, "Let's make up. We don't want to fight."
She says, "I love you more than I love you,"
    which means, according to Snoopy she
        explains, "No bombs."

Nights, I watch her sleep, the glow of new being
      rosy on her skin
her breath, strawberries in the sun.
She is healthy, bright, funny.
If we lived in other times, I would say, "Kineahora,
      let her be well,"
    as my mother before me, hers before her.
And I would take care not to brag, protecting my
      naches from the wrath
    of God or neighbors.
Yet inside I'd be smug. Contentment would tingle
      my blood like chablis.

Today I have no assurance,
only fear, fierce hope, and these precious days.
I no longer forget what is precious.

The curtain still bobs, the birds trill
the fly has chanced through the open window
and is on with its life—
maybe chances is inaccurate.
It worked, tried over and over, hurling itself against
      all surfaces until
    one did not resist and it was met by the
      familiar currents of wind

Can that happen to us?
Miracles happen. What is nature but the most
      complex, amazing miracle?

Jasmine unfolding, the scent and color attracting the
      bees,
    the darker veins guiding them toward the
        nectar,
honey in honeycombs, worms aerating soil, the
      levity of bird bones,
    fins of fish, the eye blinking—
who could have ever conceived it?
the crescent moon, tender as new love in the
      luminescent blue,
milkweed silk—who could have imagined it?

And my lover, when she lifts her lips to me and I
      first feel that softness
    warm like summer nights as a child
when she rubs against me like fur
and small cries escape my mouth like birds,
"Sing to me," she breathes
and I sing glory I did not know was mine to sing.

What is this but a miracle?
What is this but the improbable, marvelous reward
      of desire?

Desire—that fire I was taught to suspect,
    that intensity I struggled to calm.
"Don't want too much," the voices warned.

No. Want. Want life.
Want this fragile oasis of the galaxy to flourish.

Want fertility, want seasons, want this spectacular
        array of creatures,
this brilliant balance of need.

Want it. Want it all.
Desire. Welcome her raging power.
May her strength course through us.
Desire, she is life. Desire life.
Allow ourselves to desire life, to want this
        sweetness
so passionately, that we live for it.

Of a Small Daughter Walking Outdoors

FRANCES M. FROST
1905–1959

Easy, wind!
Go softly here!
She is small
And very dear.

She is young
And cannot say
Words to chase
The wind away.

She is new
To walking, so
Wind, be kind
And gently blow.

On her ruffled head,
On grass and clover.
Easy, wind . . .
She'll tumble over!

From

To Mira,
On the Care of her Infant

ANN YEARSLEY
1752–1806

Mira, as thy dear Edward's senses grow,
Be sure they all will seek this point—*to know*:
Woo to enquiry—strictures long avoid;
By force the thirst of weakly sense is cloyed:
Silent attend the frown, the gaze, the smile,
To grasp far objects the incessant toil;
So play life's springs with energy, and try
The unceasing thirst of knowledge to supply.

I saw the beauteous Caleb t' other day
Stretch forth his little hand to touch a spray,
Whilst on the grass his drowsy nurse inhaled
The sweets of Nature as her sweets exhaled:
But, ere the infant reached the playful leaf,
She pulled him back—His eyes o'erflowed with grief;
He checked his tears—Her fiercer passions strove,
She looked a vulture cowering o'er a dove!
'I'll teach you, brat!' The pretty trembler sighed—
When, with a cruel shake, she hoarsely cried—
'Your mother spoils you— every thing you see
You covet. It shall ne'er be so with me!
Here, eat this cake, sit still, and don't you rise—
Why don't you pluck the sun down from the skies?

I'll spoil your sport—Come, laugh me in the face—
And henceforth learn to keep your proper place.
You rule me in the house!—To hush your noise
I, like a spaniel, must run for toys:
But here, Sir, let the trees alone, nor cry—
Pluck if you dare—Who's master? you, or I?'
  O brutal force, to check th' enquiring mind,
When it would pleasure in a rosebud find!

Alice Clay and Sally Mitchell

MARION STROBEL MITCHELL

"Alice Clay has curls as wild
As a morning glory vine.
Oh, Alice Clay's a lovely child
But Sally Mitchell's mine.

Sally's hair is straight as hay,
And her eyes are brown, not blue—
Oh, she can't look like Alice Clay
And I don't want her to."

Lullaby

From *The Princess*

ALFRED, LORD TENNYSON
1809–1892

Sweet and low, sweet and low,
　　Wind of the western sea,
Low, low, breathe and blow,
　　Wind of the western sea!
Over the rolling waters go,
Come from the dying moon, and blow,
　　Blow him again to me;
While my little one, while my pretty one, sleeps.

Sleep and rest, sleep and rest,
　　Father will come to thee soon;
Rest, rest, on mother's breast,
　　Father will come to thee soon;
Father will come to his babe in the nest,
Silver sails all out of the west
　　Under the silver moon:
Sleep, my little one, sleep, my pretty one, sleep.

A Mother to Her Waking Infant

JOANNA BAILLIE
1762–1851

Now in thy dazzling half-oped eye,
Thy curlèd nose and lip awry,
Thy up-hoist arms and noddling head,
And little chin with chrystal spread,
Poor helpless thing! what do I see,
  That I should sing of thee?

From thy poor tongue no accents come,
Which can but rub thy toothless gum;
Small understanding boasts thy face,
Thy shapeless limbs nor step nor grace;
A few short words thy feats may tell,
  And yet I love thee well.

When sudden wakes the bitter shriek,
And redder swells thy little cheek;
When rattled keys thy woes beguile,
And through the wet eye gleams the smile,
Still for thy weakly self is spent
  Thy little silly plaint.

But when thy friends are in distress,
Thou'lt laugh and chuckle ne'er the less;
Nor e'en with sympathy be smitten,
Though all are sad but thee and kitten;
Yet little varlet that thou art,
  Thou twitchest at the heart.

Thy rosy cheek so soft and warm;
Thy pinky hand and dimpled arm;
Thy silken locks that scantly peep,
With gold-tipped ends, where circles deep
Around thy neck in harmless grace
So soft and sleekly hold their place,
Might harder hearts with kindness fill,
    And gain our right good will.

Each passing clown bestows his blessing,
Thy mouth is worn with old wives' kissing:
E'en lighter looks the gloomy eye
Of surly sense, when thou art by;
And yet I think whoe'er they be,
    They love thee not like me.

Perhaps when time shall add a few
Short years to thee, thou'lt love me too.
Then wilt thou through life's weary way
Become my sure and cheering stay:
Wilt care for me, and be my hold,
    When I am weak and old.

Thou'lt listen to my lengthened tale,
And pity me when I am frail—
But see, the sweepy spinning fly
Upon the window takes thine eye.
Go to thy little senseless play—
    Thou dost not heed my lay.

Etude Realiste

ALGERNON CHARLES SWINBURNE
1837–1909

I

A baby's feet, like sea-shells pink,
  Might tempt, should Heaven see meet,
An angel's lips to kiss, we think,
    A baby's feet.

Like rose-hued sea-flowers toward the heat
  They stretch and spread and wink
Their ten soft buds that part and meet.

No flower-bells that expand and shrink
  Gleam half so heavenly sweet
As shine on life's untrodden brink
    A baby's feet.

II

A baby's hands, like rosebuds furled,
  Whence yet no leaf expands,
Ope if you touch, though close upcurled,
    A baby's hands.

Then, even as warriors grip their brands
  When battle's bolt is hurled,
They close, clenched hard like tightening bands.

No rosebuds yet by dawn impearled
  Match, even in loveliest lands,

The sweetest flowers in all the world—
    A baby's hands.

III

A baby's eyes, ere speech begin,
    Ere lips learn words or sighs,
Bless all things bright enough to win
        A baby's eyes.

Love, while the sweet thing laughs and lies,
    And sleep flows out and in,
Lies perfect in them Paradise.

Their glance might cast out pain and sin,
    Their speech make dumb the wise,
By mute glad godhead felt within
        A baby's eyes.

Love Affair

MARGARET FISHBACK
1904–1985

Some day he'll think me rather silly,
But now he loves me willy-nilly.

There'll come a time when his inspection
Will tell him I am not perfection,

And he'll unearth some younger cutie
Who far surpasses me in beauty.

So while I have him in my arms
I'll make the most of all my charms,

And store up memories to last
When I am dwelling in the past.

For though my hold on him is strong,
He cannot stay a baby long.

The Land of Nod

ROBERT LOUIS STEVENSON
1850-1894

From breakfast on through all the day
At home among friends I stay,
But every night I go abroad
Afar into the land of Nod.

All by myself I have to go,
With none to tell me what to do—
All alone beside the streams
And up the mountainsides of dreams.

The strangest things are there for me,
Both things to eat and things to see,
And many frightening sights abroad
Till morning in the land of Nod.

Try as I like to find the way,
I never can get back by day,
Nor can remember plain and clear
The curious music that I hear.

The Gambols of Children

GEORGE DARLEY
1795–1846

Down the dimpled greensward dancing,
  Bursts a flaxen-headed bevy,—
Bud-lipt boys and girls advancing,
  Love's irregular little levy.

Rows of liquid eyes in laughter,
  How the glimmer, how they quiver!
Sparkling one another after,
  Like bright ripples on a river.

Tipsy band of rubious faces,
  Flushed with Joy's ethereal spirit,
Make your mocks and sly grimaces
  At Love's self, and do not fear it.

Like Mother, Like Son

MARGARET JOHNSTON GRAFFLIN

Do you know that your soul is of my soul such a part,
That you seem to be fibre and core of my heart?
None other can pain me as you, dear, can do,
None other can please me or praise me as you.

Remember the world will be quick with its blame
If shadow or stain ever darken your name.
"Like mother, like son" is a saying so true
The world will judge largely the "mother" by you.

Be yours then the task, if task it shall be,
To force the proud world to do homage to me.
Be sure it will say, when its verdict you've won,
"She reaped as she sowed. Lo! this is her son."

A Prayer for My Daughter

WILLIAM BUTLER YEATS
1865–1939

Once more the storm is howling, and half hid
Under this cradle-hood and coverlid
My child sleeps on. There is no obstacle
But Gregory's wood and one bare hill
Whereby the haystack- and roof-leveling wind,
Bred on the Atlantic, can be stayed;
And for an hour I have walked and prayed
Because of the great gloom that is in my mind.

I have walked and prayed for this young child an hour
And heard the sea-wind scream upon the tower,
And under the arches of the bridge, and scream
In the elms above the flooded stream;
Imagining in excited reverie
That the future years had come,
Dancing to a frenzied drum,
Out of the murderous innocence of the sea.

May she be granted beauty and yet not
Beauty to make a stranger's eye distraught,
Or hers before a looking glass, for such,
Being made beautiful overmuch,
Consider beauty a sufficient end,
Lose natural kindness and maybe
The heart-revealing intimacy
That chooses right, and never find a friend.

Helen being chosen found life flat and dull
And later had much trouble from a fool,
While that great Queen, that rose out of the spray,
Being fatherless could have her way
Yet chose a bandy-leggèd smith for man.
It's certain that fine women eat
A crazy salad with their meat,
Whereby the Horn of Plenty is undone.

In courtesy I'd have her chiefly learned;
Hearts are not had as a gift but hearts are earned
By those that are not entirely beautiful;
Yet many, that have played the fool
For beauty's very self, has charm made wise,
And many a poor man that has roved,
Loved and thought himself beloved,
From a glad kindness cannot take his eyes.

May she become a flourishing hidden tree
That all her thoughts may like the linnet be,
And have no business but dispensing round
Their magnanimities of sound,
Nor but in merriment begin a chase,
Nor but in merriment a quarrel.
Oh, may she live like some green laurel
Rooted in one dear perpetual place.

My mind, because the minds that I have loved,
The sort of beauty that I have approved,
Prosper but little, has dried up of late,
Yet knows that to be choked with hate

May well be of all evil chances chief.
If there's no hatred in a mind
Assault and battery of the wind
Can never tear the linnet from the leaf.

An intellectual hatred is the worst,
So let her think opinions are accursed.
Have I not seen the loveliest woman born
Out of the mouth of Plenty's horn,
Because of her opinionated mind
Barter that horn and every good
By quiet natures understood
For an old bellows full of angry wind?

Considering that, all hatred driven hence,
The soul recovers radical innocence
And learns at last that it is self-delighting,
Self-appeasing, self-affrighting,
And that its own sweet will is Heaven's will;
She can, though every face should scowl
And every windy quarter howl
Or every bellows burst, be happy still.

And may her bridegroom bring her to a house
Where all's accustomed, ceremonious;
For arrogance and hatred are the wares
Peddled in the thoroughfares.
How but in custom and in ceremony
Are innocence and beauty born?
Ceremony's a name for the rich horn,
And custom for the spreading laurel tree.

Willow Whistle

ETHEL ROMIG FULLER

Only a boy
Can set free
The music in
A willow tree.

Can find the cricket
And the lark
Hidden in
A willow's bark.

Can fife and flute,
Can lilt and croon
The notes that make
A willow tune.

Can blow an air
Winged as a thistle
From a little
Willow whistle.

Polly

WILLIAM BRIGHTLY HANDS

Brown eyes,
   Straight nose;
Dirt pies,
   Rumpled clothes;

Torn books,
   Spoiled toys;
Arch looks,
   Unlike a boy's;

Little rages,
   Obvious arts;
(Three her age is),
   Cakes, tarts;

Falling down
   Off chairs;
Breaking crown
   Down stairs;

Catching flies
   On the pane;
Deep sighs,—
   Cause not plain;

Bribing you
    With kisses
For a few
    Farthing blisses;

Wide awake,
    As you hear,
"Mercy's sake,
    Quiet, dear!"

New shoes,
    New frock,
Vague views
    Of what's o'clock,

When it's time
    To go to bed,
And scorn sublime
    For what it said;

Folded hands,
    Saying prayers,
Understands
    Not, nor cares;

Thinks it odd,
    Smiles away;
Yet may God
    Hear her pray!

Bedgown white,
　Kiss Dolly;
Good-night!—
　That's Polly.

Fast asleep,
　As you see;
Heaven keep
　My girl for me!

Ceiling Zero

MARGARET FISHBACK
1904–1985

Though, as a housewife, I deplore
The traffic that congests our floor—
The Army trucks, the trains, the tracks,
The trolley, and the boy scout ax,
I rather think, without the mess
I'd ache with empty loneliness,
But even so, it seems to rankle
Each time I trip and sprain an ankle.

The Reading Mother

STRICKLAND W. GILLILAN
1869–1954

I had a Mother who read to me
Sagas of pirates who scoured the sea,
Cutlasses clenched in their yellow teeth,
"Blackbirds" stowed in the hold beneath.

I had a Mother who read me lays
Of ancient and gallant and golden days;
Stories of Marmion and Ivanhoe,
Which every boy has a right to know.

I had a Mother who read me tales
Of Gelert the hound of the hills of Wales,
True to his trust till his tragic death,
Faithfulness blent with his final breath.

I had a Mother who read me the things
That wholesome life to the boy heart brings—
Stories that stir with an upward touch,
Oh, that each mother of boys were such!

You may have tangible wealth untold;
Caskets of jewels and coffers of gold.
Richer than I you can never be—
I had a Mother who read to me.

Wha Me Mudder Do

GRACE NICHOLS
1950–

Mek me tell you wha me Mudder do
wha me mudder do
wha me mudder do

Me mudder pound plantain mek fufu
Me mudder catch crab mek calaloo stew

Mek me tell you wha me mudder do
wha me mudder do
wha me mudder do

Me mudder beat hammer
Me mudder turn screw
she paint chair red
then she paint it blue

Mek me tell you wha me mudder do
wha me mudder do
wha me mudder do

Me mudder chase bad-cow
with one 'Shoo'
she paddle down river
in she own canoe

Ain't have nothing
dat me mudder can't do
Ain't have nothing
dat me mudder can't do

Mek me tell you

Children

WALTER SAVAGE LANDOR
1775–1864

Children are what the mothers are.
No fondest father's fondest care
Can fashion so the infant heart
As those creative beams that dart,
With all their hopes and fears, upon
The cradle of a sleeping son.

His startled eyes with wonder see
A father near him on his knee,
Who wishes all the while to trace
The mother in his future face;
But 't is to her alone uprise
His waking arms; to her those eyes
Open with joy and not surprise.

Little Boys

MARGARETTA SCOTT

I like rumpled little boys
With collars upstanding,
And buttons missing:
Little boys with rough, red cheeks,
And freckled noses,
And restless hands
That are never still.

I like neat little boys
In Norfolk suits,
With white collars and dotted Windsor ties,
Little boys with shining, soapy faces,
And slicked back hair, still wet,
And restless hands
That are never still.
I like little boys.

Three Poems for Women

SUSAN GRIFFIN

1953–

This is a poem for a woman doing dishes.
This is a poem for a woman doing dishes.
It must be repeated.
It must be repeated,
again and again,
again and again,
because the woman doing dishes
because the woman doing dishes
has trouble hearing
has trouble hearing.

And this is another poem for a woman
cleaning the floor
who cannot hear at all.
Let us have a moment of silence
for the woman who cleans the floor.

And here is one more poem
for the woman at home
with children.
You never see her at night.
Stare at an empty space and imagine her there,
the woman with children
because she cannot be here to speak
for herself,
and listen
to what you think
she might say.

"Where's Mamma?"

Edgar A. Guest
1881–1959

Comes in flying from the street:
　　"Where's Mamma?"
Friend or stranger thus he'll greet:
　　"Where's Mamma?"
Doesn't want to say hello,
Home from school or play he'll go
Straight to what he wants to know;
　　"Where's Mamma?"

Many times a day he'll shout,
　　"Where's Mamma?"
Seems afraid that she's gone out;
　　"Where's Mamma?"
Is his first thought at the door
She's the one he's looking for,
And he questions o'er and o'er,
　　"Where's Mamma?"

Can't be happy till he knows:
　　"Where's Mamma?"
So he begs us to disclose
　　"Where's Mamma?"
And it often seems to me,
As I hear his anxious plea,
That no sweeter phrase can be:
　　"Where's Mamma?"

Like to hear it day by day:
    "Where's Mamma?"
Loveliest phrase that lips can say:
    "Where's Mamma?"
And I pray as time shall flow,
And the long years come and go,
That he'll always want to know
    "Where's Mamma?"

Mother's Song

ANONYMOUS

If snow falls on the far field
where travelers
spend the night,
I ask you, cranes,
to warm my child in your wings.

Translated by Willis Barnstone

The Land of Storybooks

ROBERT LOUIS STEVENSON
1850–1894

At evening when the lamp is lit,
Around the fire my parents sit;
They sit at home and talk and sing,
And do not play at anything.

Now, with my little gun, I crawl
All in the dark along the wall,
And follow round the forest track
Away behind the sofa back.

There, in the night, where none can spy,
All in my hunter's camp I lie,
And play at books that I have read
Till it is time to go to bed.

These are the hills, there are the woods,
These are my starry solitudes;
And there the river by whose brink
The roaring lions come to drink.

I see the others far away
As if in firelit camp they lay,
And I, like to an Indian scout,
Around their party prowled about.

So, when my nurse comes in for me,
Home I return across the sea,
And go to bed with backward looks
At my dear land of Storybooks.

To a Small City Slicker

MARGARET FISHBACK
1904–1985

Dear little human dynamo
Perpetually on the go,
Your hummingbird vitality
Amazes and bedevils me.

With puckered brow and aching feet,
I chase you up and down the street.
God gave you something to be sat on,
But you must cover all Manhattan.

You're bored, parading in your pram.
At large, you're happy as a clam.
Oh, for a yard to set you loose,
And let me rest on my caboose!

A Dutch Lullaby

EUGENE FIELD
1850–1895

Wynken, Blynken, and Nod one night
   Sailed off in a wooden shoe—
Sailed on a river of misty light
   Into a sea of dew.
"Where are you going, and what do you wish?"
   The old moon asked the three.
"We have come to fish for the herring-fish
   That live in this beautiful sea;
   Nets of silver and gold have we,"
         Said Wynken,
         Blynken,
         And Nod.

The old moon laughed and sung a song
   As they rocked in the wooden shoe,
And the wind that sped them all night long
   Ruffled the waves of dew;
The little stars were the herring-fish
   That lived in the beautiful sea;
"Now cast your nets wherever you wish,
   But never afeard are we"—
   So cried the stars to the fishermen three,
         Wynken,
         Blynken,
         And Nod.

All night long their nets they threw
  For the fish in the twinkling foam,
Then down from the sky came the wooden shoe,
  Bringing the fishermen home.
'T was all so pretty a sail, it seemed
  As if it could not be;
And some folks thought 't was a dream they'd
      dreamed
  Of sailing that beautiful sea.
  But I shall name you the fishermen three:
          Wynken,
          Blynken,
          And Nod.

Wynken and Blynken are two little eyes,
  And Nod is a little head,
And the wooden shoe that sailed the skies
  Is a wee one's trundle-bed;
So shut your eyes while mother sings
  Of the wonderful sights that be,
And you shall see the beautiful things
  As you rock in the misty sea
  Where the old shoe rocked the fishermen three—
          Wynken,
          Blynken,
          And Nod.

Baby Running Barefoot

D. H. LAWRENCE
1885–1930

When the white feet of the baby beat across the grass
The little white feet nod like white flowers in a wind,
They poise and run like puffs of wind that pass
Over water where the weeds are thinned.

And the sight of their white playing in the grass
Is winsome as a robin's song, so fluttering;
Or like two butterflies that settle on a glass
Cup for a moment, soft little wing-beats uttering.

And I wish that the baby would tack across here to me
Like a wind-shadow running on a pond, so she could
    stand
With two little bare white feet upon my knee
And I could feel her feet in either hand

Cool as syringa buds in morning hours,
Or firm and silken as young peony flowers.

Candida

PATRICK KAVANAGH
1905–1967

For John Betjeman's Daughter

Candida is one to-day,
What is there that *one* can say?
One is where the race begins
Or the sum that counts our sins;
But the mark time makes to-morrow
Shapes the cross of joy or sorrow.

Candida is one to-day,
What is there for me to say?
On the day that she was one
There were apples in the sun
And the fields long wet with rain
Crumply in dry winds again.

Candida is one and I
Wish her lots and lots of joy.
She the nursling of September
Like a war she won't remember.
Candida is one to-day
And there's nothing more to say.

On My Own Little Daughter, Four Years Old

ANONYMOUS

1798

Sweet lovely infant, innocently gay,
  With blooming face arrayed in peaceful smiles,
How light thy cheerful heart doth sportive play,
  Unconscious of all future cares and toils.

With what delight I've seen thy little feet
  Dancing with pleasure at my near approach!
Eager they ran my well-known form to meet,
  Secure of welcome, fearless of reproach.

Then happy hast thou prattled in mine ear
  Thy little anxious tales of pain or joy;
Thy fears lest faithful Tray thy frock should tear,
  Thy pride when ladies give the gilded toy.

How oft, when sad reflection dimmed mine eye,
  As memory recalled past scenes of woe,
Thy tender heart hath heaved the expressive sigh
  Of sympathy, for ills thou could'st not know.

Oft too in silence I've admired that face,
  Beaming with pity for a mother's grief,
Whilst in each anxious feature I could trace
  Compassion eager to afford relief.

E'en now methinks I hear that artless tongue,
    Lisping sweet sounds of comfort to mine ear:
'Oh! fret no more—your Fanny is not gone—
    She will not go—don't cry—your Fanny's here.'

If, ere her mind attains its full-grown strength,
    Thy will consigns me to an early tomb,
If in Thy sight my thread's near run its length,
    And called by Thee I cannot watch her bloom—

Oh heavenly Father, guard my infant child;
    Protect her steps through this wide scene of care;
Within her breast implant each virtue mild,
    And teach her all she ought to hope or fear.

To My Mother

ROBERT LOUIS STEVENSON
1850–1894

You too, my mother, read my rhymes
For love of unforgotten times,
And you may chance to hear once more
The little feet along the floor.

The Country Child

KATHARINE TYNAN HINKSON
1861–1931

The Country Child has fragrances
   He breathes about him as he goes;
Clear eyes that look at distances,
   And in his cheek the wilding rose.

The sun, the sun himself will stain
   The country face to its own red,
The red-gold of the ripening grain,
   And bleach to white the curly head.

He rises to the morning lark,
   Sleeps with the evening primroses,
Before the curtain of the dark
   Lets down its splendour, starred with bees.

He sleeps so sweet without a dream
   Under brown cottage eaves and deep,
His window holds one stray moonbeam
   As though an angel kept his sleep.

He feeds on honest country fare,
   Drinks the clear water of the spring;
Green carpets wait him everywhere,
   Where he may run, where he may sing.

He hath his country lore by heart,
    And what is friend and what is foe;
Hath conned Dame Nature's book apart—
    Her child since he began to grow.

When he is old, when he goes sad,
    Hobbling upon a twisted knee,
He keeps somewhat of joys he had,
    Since an old countryman is he.

He keeps his childhood's innocencies,
    Though his old head be bleached to snow.
Forget-me-nots still hold his eyes,
    And in his cheeks old roses blow.

The Parent

OGDEN NASH
1902–1971

Children aren't happy with nothing to ignore,
And that's what parents were created for.

Greenwich Village Baby

JUDITH VIORST
1931–

Irvington children are usually Peters and Debbies
Who eat Cap'n Crunch in vinyl dining areas.
Go to Radio City Music Hall in car pools.
And brush after every meal.

That is not the kind of child I have in mind.

Someday I'll have a Greenwich Village baby,
The kind who likes Vivaldi when he's three.
Has too much hair, no shoes, a high IQ,
And his own analyst.

I'll feed my baby Camembert and paté.
He'll only watch the finest N.E.T.,
While his father—the poet—sits in a sling chair
Writing a sonnet.

I will not raise my son to be a doctor.
He will not have to love his dad or me.
I'll be content with any girl he chooses,
As long as she pickets.

Someday I'll have a Greenwich Village baby,
At seventeen he'll have his Ph.D.
At twenty-five his Andrea and Luke
Will play in the sandbox at Washington Square
While their grandmother—the medieval scholar—
Sits on a bench
Reading Aquinas in Latin.

A Cradle Song

WILLIAM BUTLER YEATS
1865–1939

*'Coth yani me von gilli beg,
'N heur ve thu more a creena.'*

The angels are bending
   Above your white bed,
They weary of tending
   The souls of the dead.

God smiles in high heaven
   To see you so good,
The old planets seven
   Grow gay with his mood.

I kiss you and kiss you,
   With arms round my own,
Ah, how shall I miss you,
   When, dear, you have grown.

Cuddle Doon

ALEXANDER ANDERSON
1794–1869

The bairnies cuddle doon at nicht
　Wi' muckle faught an' din;
"Oh try and sleep, ye waukrife rogues,
　Your faither 's comin' in."
They never heed a word I speak;
　I try to gie a froon,
But aye I hap them up an' cry,
　"Oh, bairnies, cuddle doon."

Wee Jamie wi' the curly heid—
　He aye sleeps next the wa'—
Bangs up an' cries, "I want a piece;"
　The rascal starts them a'.
I rin an' fetch them pieces, drinks,
　They stop awee the soun',
Then draw the blankets up an' cry,
　"Noo, weanies, cuddle doon."

But, ere five minutes gang, wee Rab
　Cries out, frae 'neath the claes,
"Mither, mak' Tam gie ower at ance,
　He 's kittlin' wi' his taes."
The mischief 's in that Tam for tricks,
　He 'd bother half the toon;
But aye I hap them up and cry,
　"Oh, bairnies, cuddle doon."

112

At length they hear their faither's fit,
　　An', as he steeks the door,
They turn their faces to the wa',
　　While Tam pretends to snore.
"Hae a' the weans been gude?" he asks,
　　As he pits aff his shoon;
"The bairnies, John, are in their beds,
　　An' lang since cuddled doon."

An' just afore we bed oorsels,
　　We look at our wee lambs;
Tam has his airm roun' wee Rab's neck,
　　And Rab his airm round Tam's.
I lift wee Jamie up the bed,
　　An' as I straik each croon,
I whisper, till my heart fills up,
　　"Oh, bairnies, cuddle doon."

The bairnies cuddle doon at nicht
　　Wi' mirth that 's dear to me;
But soon the big warl's cark an' care
　　Will quaten doon their glee.
Yet, come what will to ilka ane,
　　May He who rules aboon
Aye whisper, though their pows be bald,
　　"Oh, bairnies, cuddle doon."

The Children and Sir Nameless

THOMAS HARDY
1840–1928

Sir Nameless, once of Athelhall, declared:
"These wretched children romping in my park
Trample the herbage till the soil is bared,
And yap and yell from early morn till dark!
Go keep them harnessed to their set routines:
Thank God I've none to hasten my decay;
For green remembrance there are better means
Than offspring, who but wish their sires away."

Sir Nameless of that mansion said anon:
"To be perpetuate for my mightiness
Sculpture must image me when I am gone."
—He forthwith summoned carvers there express
To shape a figure stretching seven-odd feet
(For he was tall) in alabaster stone,
With shield, and crest, and casque, and sword complete:
When done a statelier work was never known.

Three hundred years hied; Church-restorers came,
And, no one of his lineage being traced,
They thought an effigy so large in frame
Best fitted for the floor. There it was placed,
Under the seats for schoolchildren. And they
Kicked out his name, and hobnailed off his nose;
And, as they yawn through sermon-time, they say,
"Who was this old stone man beneath our toes?"

Little Rose

From *Blackwood's Magazine*

She comes with fairy footsteps;
  Softly their echoes fall;
And her shadow plays, like a summer shade,
  Across the garden wall.
The golden light is dancing bright
  Mid the mazes of her hair,
And her fair young locks are waving free
  To the wooing of the air.

Like a sportive fawn she boundeth
  So gleefully along;
As a wild young bird she caroleth
  The burden of a song.
The summer birds are clustering thick
  Around her dancing feet,
And on her cheek the clustering breeze
  Is breaking soft and sweet.

The very sunbeams seem to linger
  Above that holy head,
And the wild flowers at her coming
  Their richest fragrance shed.
And O, how lovely light and fragrance
  Mingle in the life within!
O, how fondly do they nestle
  Round the soul that knows no sin!

She comes, the spirit of our childhood,—
   A thing of mortal birth,
Yet beareth still a breath of heaven,
   To redeem her from the earth.
She comes in bright-robed innocence,
   Unsoiled by blot or blight,
And passeth by our wayward path
   A gleam of angel light.

O, blessed things are children!
   The gifts of heavenly love;
They stand betwixt our heavenly hearts
   And better things above.
They link us with the spirit world
   By purity and truth,
And keep our hearts still fresh and young
   With the presence of their youth.

Song

E. NESBIT
1858–1924

Oh, baby, baby, baby dear,
We lie along together here;
The snowy gown and cap and sheet
With lavender are fresh and sweet;

116

Through half-closed blinds the roses peer
To see and love you, baby dear.

We are so tired, we like to lie
Just doing nothing, you and I,
Within the darkened quiet room.
The sun sends dusk rays through the gloom,
Which is no gloom since you are here,
My little life, my baby dear.

Soft sleepy mouth so vaguely pressed
Against your new-made mother's breast.
Soft little hands in mine I fold,
Soft little feet I kiss and hold,
Round soft smooth head and tiny ear,
All mine, my own, my baby dear.

And he we love is far away!
But he will come some happy day,
You need but me, and I can rest
At peace with you beside me pressed.
There are no questions, longings vain,
No murmuring, nor doubt, nor pain,
Only content and we are here,
          My baby dear.

Nobody Knows But Mother

MARY MORRISON

How many buttons are missing today?
Nobody knows but Mother.
How many playthings are strewn in her way?
Nobody knows but Mother.
How many thimbles and spools has she missed?
How many burns on each fat little fist?
How many bumps to be cuddled and kissed?
Nobody knows but Mother.

How many hats has she hunted today?
Nobody knows but Mother.
Carelessly hiding themselves in the hay—
Nobody knows but Mother.
How many handkerchiefs wilfully strayed?
How many ribbons for each little maid?
How for her care can a mother be paid?
Nobody knows but Mother.

How many muddy shoes all in a row?
Nobody knows but Mother.
How many stockings to darn, do you know?
Nobody knows but Mother.
How many little torn aprons to mend?
How many hours of toil must she spend?
What is the time when her day's work shall end?
Nobody knows but Mother.

How many lunches for Tommy and Sam?
  Nobody knows but Mother.
Cookies and apples and blackberry jam—
  Nobody knows but Mother.
Nourishing dainties for every "sweet tooth,"
Toddling Dottie or dignified Ruth—
How much love sweetens the labor, forsooth?
  Nobody knows but Mother.

How many cares does a mother's heart know?
  Nobody knows but Mother.
How many joys from her mother love flow?
  Nobody knows but Mother.
How many prayers for each little white bed?
How many tears for her babes has she shed?
How many kisses for each curly head?
  Nobody knows but Mother.

Children Are Color-Blind

GENNY LIM

1946–

I never painted myself yellow
the way I colored the sun when I was five.
The way I colored whitefolks with the "flesh" crayola.
Yellow pages adults thumbed through for restaurants,
taxis, airlines, plumbers . . .
The color of summer squash, corn, eggyolk, innocence
       and tapioca.

My children knew before they were taught.
They envisioned rainbows emblazoned over alleyways;
Clouds floating over hilltops like a freedom shroud.
With hands clasped, time dragged them along and they
       followed.

Wind-flushed cheeks persimmon,
eyes dilated like dark pearls staring out the backseat
       windows,
they speed through childhood like greyhounds
into the knot of night, hills fanning out,
an ocean ending at an underpass,
a horizon blunted by lorries, skyscrapers,
vision blurring at the brink of poverty.

Dani, my three-year-old, recites the alphabet from
billboards flashing by like pages of a cartoon flipbook,
where above, carpetbaggers patrol the freeways like

Olympic gods hustling their hi-tech neon gospel,
looking down from the fast lane,
dropping Kool dreams, booze dreams, fancy car dreams,
fast food dreams, sex dreams and no-tomorrow dreams
like eight balls into your easy psychic pocket.

"Only girls with black hair, black eyes can join!"
My eight-year-old was chided at school for excluding a
        blonde
from her circle. "Only girls with black hair, black eyes
can join!" taunted the little Asian girls, black hair,
black eyes flashing, mirroring, mimicking what they
        heard
as the message of the medium, the message of the world-
        at-large:
    "Apartheid, segregation, self-determination!
    Segregation, apartheid, revolution!"
Like a contrapuntal hymn, like a curse that refrains in a
        melody trapped.
Sometimes at night I touch the children when they're
        sleeping
and the coolness of my fingers sends shivers through
        them that
is a foreshadowing, a guilt imparted.

Dani doesn't paint herself yellow
the way I colored the sun.
The way she dances in its light as I watch from the
        shadow.
No, she says green is her favorite color.
"It's the color of life!"

121

The World Is with Me Just Enough

SAM ABRAMS
1935–

my seven year old friend
visited & tickled me
for an hour nearly

who needs the national
academy of arts & sciences

i'd rather be a pagan
tickled in a creed outworn

hurrah for alexa flaherty
mother of arts sciences magics
religions economics states
theories giggles

& of all these
the greatest is the last
by far

A Portrait

ELIZABETH BARRETT BROWNING
1806–1861

"One name is Elizabeth."
—*Ben Jonson.*

I will paint her as I see her.
Ten times have the lilies blown
Since she looked upon the sun.

And her face is lily-clear,
Lily-shaped, and dropped in duty
To the law of its own beauty.

Oval cheeks encolored faintly,
Which a trail of golden hair
Keeps from fading off to air;

And a forehead fair and saintly
Which two blue eyes undershine,
Like meek prayers before a shrine.

Face and figure of a child,—
Though too calm, you think, and tender,
For the childhood you would lend her.

Yet child-simple, undefiled,
Frank, obedient,—waiting still
On the turnings of your will.

Moving light, as all your things,
  As young birds, or early wheat,
  When the wind blows over it.

Only, free from flutterings
  Of loud mirth that scorneth measure,—
  Taking love for her chief pleasure.

Choosing pleasures, for the rest,
  Which come softly,—just as she,
  When she nestles at your knee.

Quiet talk she liketh best,
  In a bower of gentle looks,—
  Watering flowers, or reading books.

And her voice, it murmurs lowly,
  As a silver stream may run,
  Which yet feels, you feel, the sun.

And her smile, it seems half holy,
  As if drawn from thoughts more far
  Than our common jestings are.

And if any poet knew her,
  He would sing of her with falls
  Used in lovely madrigals.

And if any painter drew her,
  He would paint her unaware
  With a halo round the hair.

And if reader read the poem,
　　He would whisper, "You have done a
　　Consecrated little Una."

And a dreamer (did you show him
　　That same picture) would exclaim,
　　"'T is my angel, with a name!"

And a stranger, when he sees her
　　In the street even, smileth stilly,
　　Just as you would at a lily.

And all voices that address her
　　Soften, sleeken every word,
　　As if speaking to a bird.

And all fancies yearn to cover
　　The hard earth whereon she passes,
　　With the thymy-scented grasses.

And all hearts do pray, "God love her!"—
　　Ay, and always, in good sooth,
　　We may all be sure He doth.

For the Children

GARY SNYDER
1930–

The rising hills, the slopes,
of statistics
lie before us.
the steep climb
of everything, going up,
up, as we all
go down.

In the next century
or the one beyond that,
they say,
are valleys, pastures,
we can meet there in peace
if we make it.

To climb these coming crests
one word to you, to
you and your children:

stay together
learn the flowers
go light

Written for My Son, and Spoken by Him on His First Putting on Breeches

MARY BARBER

c. 1690–1757

What is it our mammas bewitches,
To plague us little boys with breeches?
To tyrant Custom we must yield
Whilst vanquished Reason flies the field,
Our legs must suffer by ligation,
To keep the blood from circulation;
And then our feet, though young and tender,
We to the shoemaker surrender,
Who often makes our shoes so strait
Our growing feet they cramp and fret;
Whilst, with contrivance most profound,
Across our insteps we are bound;
Which is the cause, I make no doubt,
Why thousands suffer in the gout.
Our wiser ancestors wore brogues,
Before the surgeons bribed these rogues,
With narrow toes, and heels like pegs,
To help to make us break our legs.

Then, ere we know to use our fists,
Our mothers closely bind our wrists;
And never think our clothes are neat,
Till they're so tight we cannot eat.

And, to increase our other pains,
That hat-band helps to cramp our brains,
The cravat finishes the work,
Like bowstring sent from the Grand Turk.

Thus dress, that should prolong our date,
Is made to hasten on our fate.
Fair privilege of nobler natures,
To be more plagued than other creatures!
The wild inhabitants of air
Are clothed by heaven with wondrous care:
The beauteous, well-compacted feathers
Are coats of mail against all weathers;
Enamelled, to delight the eye,
Gay as the bow that decks the sky.
The beasts are clothed with beauteous skins;
The fishes armed with scales and fins,
Whose lustre lends the sailor light,
When all the stars are hid in night.

O were our dress contrived like these,
For use, for ornament and ease!
Man only seems to sorrow born,
Naked, defenceless and forlorn.

Yet we have Reason, to supply
What nature did to man deny:
Weak viceroy! Who thy power will own,
When Custom has usurped thy throne?
In vain did I appeal to thee,

Ere I would wear his livery;
Who, in defiance to thy rules,
Delights to make us act like fools.
O'er human race the tyrant reigns,
And binds them in eternal chains.
We yield to his despotic sway,
The only monarch all obey.

Response

BOB KAUFMAN
1925–1986

For Eileen

Sleep, little one, sleep for me,
Sleep the deep sleep of love.
You are loved, awake or dreaming,
You are loved.

Dancing winds will sing for you,
Ancient gods will pray for you,
A poor lost poet will love you,
As stars appear
In the dark
Skies.

Wee Willie Winkie

WILLIAM MILLER
1810–1872

Wee Willie Winkie rins through the town,
Up stairs and doon stairs in his nicht-gown,
Tirling at the windows, crying at the lock,
Are the weans in their bed, for it's now ten o'clock?

Hey, Willie Winkie, are ye coming ben?
The cat's singing grey thrums to the sleeping hen,
The dog's spelder'd on the floor, and disna gi'e a cheep,
But here's a waukrife laddie! that winna fa' asleep.

Onything but sleep, you rogue! glow'ring like the moon,
Rattling in an airn jug wi' an airn spoon,
Rumbling, tumbling round about, crawing like a cock,
Skirling like a kenna-what, wauk'ning sleeping fock.

Hey, Willie Winkie—the wean's in a creel!
Wambling aff a bodie's knee like a very eel,
Rugging at the cat's lug, and raveling a' her thrums
Hey, Willie Winkie—see, there he comes!

Wearied is the mither that has a stoorie wean,
A wee stumpie stoussie, that canna rin his lane,
That has a battle aye wi' sleep before he'll close an ee—
But a kiss frae aff his rosy lips gi'es strength anew to me.

Castles in the Air

JAMES BALLANTINE
1808–1877

The bonnie, bonnie bairu sits pokin' in the ase,
Glowerin' the fire wi' his wee round face;
Laughin' at the fuffin' lowe—what sees he there?
Ha! the young dreamer's biggin' castles in the air!

His wee chubby face, an' his tousy curly pow,
Are laughin' an' noddin' to the dancin' lowe,
He'll brown his rosy cheeks, and singe his sunny hair,
Glow'rin' at the imps wi' their castles in the air.

He sees muckle castles towerin' to the moon.
He sees little sodgers pu'in' them a' doun;
Warlds whomlin' up an' doun, bleezin' wi' a flare,
Losh! how he loups, as they glimmer in the air!

For a' sae sage he looks, what can the laddie ken?
He's thinkin' upon naething, like mony mighty men.
A wee thing mak's us think, a sma' thing mak's us stare,
There are mair folks than him biggin' castles in the air.

Sic a night in winter may weel mak him cauld;
His chin upon his buffy hand will soon mak him auld;
His brow is brent sae braid, so pray that Daddy Care
Wad let the wean alane wi' his castles in the air.

He'll glower at the fire, and he'll keek at the light;
But mony sparkling stars are swallow'd up by Night;
Aulder een than his are glamour'd by a glare,
Hearts are broken—heads are turned—wi' castles in the
   air.

album

LUCILLE CLIFTON
1936–

for lucille chan hall

1.   it is 1939.
     our mothers are turning our hair
     around rags.
     our mothers
     have filled our shirley temple cups.
     we drink it all.

2.   1939 again.
     our shirley temple curls.
     shirley yellow.
     shirley black.
     our colors are fading.

later we had to learn ourselves.
back across 2 oceans
into bound feet and nappy hair.

3. 1958 and 9.
   we have dropped daughters,
   afrikan and chinese.
   we think
   they will be beautiful.
   we think
   they will become themselves.

4. it is 1985.
   she is.
   she is.
   they are.

Cradle Song

ALICE CARY
1820–1871

All by the sides of the wide wild river
   Surging sad through the sodden land,
There be the black reeds washing together—
   Washing together in rain and sand;
Going, blowing, flowing, together—
   Rough are the winds, and the tide runs high—
Hush little babe in thy silken cradle—
   Lull lull, lull lull, lull lullaby!

Father is riding home, little baby,
   Riding home through the wind and rain;
Flinty hoofs on the flag stems beating
   Thrum like a flail on the golden grain.
All in the wild, wet reeds of the lowlands,
Dashed and plashed with the freezing foam,
There be the blood-red wings of the starlings
   Shining to light and lead him home.

Spurring hard o'er the grass-gray ridges—
   Washing together in rain and sand,
Down of the yellow-throated creeper—
   Plumes of the woodcock, green and black—
Boughs of salix, and combs of honey—
   These be the gifts he is bearing back.

Yester morning four sweet ground-doves
   Sung so gay to their nest in the wall—
Oh, by the moaning, and oh, by the droning,
   The wild, wild water is over them all!
Come, O morning, come with thy roses,
   Flame like a burning bush in the sky—
Hush, little babe, in thy silken cradle—
   Lull lull, lull lull, lull lullaby!

My Mother

JANE TAYLOR
1783–1824

Who fed me from her gentle breast
And hushed me in her arms to rest,
And on my cheek sweet kisses prest?
　　　My mother.

When sleep forsook my open eye,
Who was it sung sweet lullaby
And rocked me that I should not cry?
　　　My mother.

Who sat and watched my infant head
When sleeping in my cradle bed,
And tears of sweet affection shed?
　　　My mother.

When pain and sickness made me cry,
Who gazed upon my heavy eye
And wept, for fear that I should die?
　　　My mother.

Who ran to help me when I fell
And would some pretty story tell,
Or kiss the part to make it well?
　　　My mother.

Who taught my infant lips to pray,
To love God's holy word and day,
And walk in wisdom's pleasant way?
      My mother.

And can I ever cease to be
Affectionate and kind to thee
Who wast so very kind to me,—
      My mother.

Oh no, the thought I cannot bear;
And if God please my life to spare
I hope I shall reward thy care,
      My mother.

When thou art feeble, old and gray,
My healthy arm shall be thy stay,
And I will soothe thy pains away,
      My mother.

And when I see thee hang thy head,
'Twill be my turn to watch thy bed,
And tears of sweet affection shed,—
      My mother.

Gifts

KAREN SNOW
1923–

Transient Americans,
Here we are once more,
coaxing our burden of possessions
into yet another house . . .
ruthlessly junking the excess.
But two treasures we'll never relinquish:

This bright blue ceramic thing
spotted with orange. It could be
a stubby snake with a thimble-bonnet
in place of a head. Or maybe the
carbon-smeared cavity makes it a
chubby tobacco pipe?

. . . and this mother-of-pearl lined
wooden leaf dish the size of my palm.

The sooty snake-pipe ringed with oozed
glue is our much-mended candle-snuffer.
Aran, age ten, made it for me.

After Thanksgiving dinner, when I blew out
the candles, my husband, Malcolm, scolded,
"Now look what you've done to this teak table."
Contrite, I said, "I need a candle-snuffer."
Aran touched the wax tears. "Mom, what's a
candle-snuffer?"

With an inverted spoon over the smoking
black wick, I demonstrated.

A week later, Aran entered the kitchen,
grinning, his whole face singing,
his extended arm singing,
and I took from his palm the Kleenex-
swaddled packet   and unveiled this
clay candle-snuffer   and the whole
kitchen was caroling.

In that moment, Aran was my father,
and it was my seventh birthday.
Grinning like Will Rogers, he was extending
a newspaper bundle toward me,
and wonky from measles, I saw in the core
three pink flowers such as I'd never seen
before   blossoms like baby cheeks
among quivering damp ferns. "Lady's-slippers,"
Daddy said, "from the marsh alongside the track."

"That's railroad property!" Mamma flailed.
"That's stealing!"
Pushing up his hat—just like Will Rogers—
Daddy handed me the bundle. "You hold them,
Mina, and I'll get the spade." And I watched
the bouquet, all but breathing.
"You can't transplant those," Mamma sputtered.
"They'll die. The sun."

Cradling the flowers, I followed my dad to the
north side of the house, where nothing grew.
"Get in here, Mina!" Mamma fussed. "The light.
I *told* you. Your eyes."
But I stood beside my dad while
He transplanted the flowers.

And every day I watered them.

"They won't come up next year," Mamma would
nag. "Don't be surprised if the neighbors
notify the police."

But they were up for my eighth birthday,
(I hadn't gone blind, and the cops never came.)
larger than before   plus a satiny white star
"A trillium," Daddy told me, and a small yellow
lady's slipper, "or orchid," he said.
"Well, don't count on it next year," Mamma lashed.
She had flogged a piñata.

May after May
under papermill soot and Mamma's hectoring
and freight train smoke   the beauties sprang
up   bountifully   and always the bonus twins.
Seven   nine   eleven   lush pink pouches
and trilliums and yellow orchids.

Now for the leaf-shaped dish.

Scowling at a windowfull of these in an
imports shop newly opened in our suburb,
Malcolm scoffed, "Trash. I'd like to see
a stiff tariff slapped on those peon products."

A week later: December snowstorm, twilight
growing into dark. Tad's baked potato is
wrinkling in the warm oven. I'm wringing
my hands. Where IS that boy?

A stomping. A thumping. It's Tad,
his fair fleece snow-soaked, a soggy
brown sack in his blue clutch.
"Come here, Mom," he whispers, and I
follow his drowned shoes up the stairs.
His eyes gleaming like a saint's his
stiff suffering hand extracts from the sack
"It's for Dad." the leaf dish. "Hand-made
in India. *Pearl!*"

I was in the presence of Galahad and the holy grail.

I perch the leaf dish, as always,
on the top shelf of Malcolm's desk
in company with the Noh mask and African
ivory and Chinese Jade.
The candle-snuffer presides here,
between Malcolm's heirloom Haviland
and silver candlesticks.

I think of our lineage, usually,
as a skein of protein so widging and
widdershins that it's sagging towards
extinction.
I had forgotten these filaments that
flame forth, seasonally, to plait us into
the broad braid of humanity.

Only yesterday, Aran's girl-wife,
glancing toward the ceiling where the
bald light bulb had recently glared,
announced, shyly, to us, her brittle guests,
"Aran stayed up half the night making this—"
And the woven willow lampshade floated over
our Thanksgiving feast   like an angel.

We surmount our spoilers, sometimes.

ACKNOWLEDGMENTS

"album" by Lucille Clifton © 1987 by Lucille Clifton. Reprinted from *Next* by Lucille Clifton, with the permission of BOA Editions, Ltd., 92 Park Ave., Brockport, NY 14420

"Alive" by Judith Wright from *Collected Poems*. © Judith Wright 1994. Reprinted by permission of HarperCollinsPublishers Australia.

"The Anatomy of Melancholy" by Margaret Fishback from *Look Who's a Mother!* Copyright © 1945 by Margaret Fishback. Copyright renewed © 1972 by Margaret Fishback. Reprinted by permission of Simon & Schuster, Inc.

"The Baby" by George MacDonald from *The World's Best Poetry*, volume I, Home/Friendship, edited by Bliss Carman. Copyright © 1981 by Granger Book Co., Inc. Reprinted by permission of Roth Publishing Inc.

"Baby Feet" from *Collected Verse of Edgar A. Guest*. Copyright © 1934 by Contemporary Books, Inc. Reprinted by permission of the publisher.

"Baby Running Barefoot" by D. H. Lawrence from *The Complete Poems of D. H. Lawrence* by D. H. Lawrence, edited by V. de Sola Pinto & F. W. Roberts. Copyright © 1964, 1971 by Angelo

Ravagli and C. M. Weekley, Executors of the Estate of Frieda Lawrence Ravagli. Used by permission of Viking Penguin, a division of Penguin Books USA Inc.

"Birth" by Annie R. Stillman from *The World's Best Poetry*, volume I, Home/Friendship, edited by Bliss Carman. Copyright © 1981 by Granger Book Co., Inc. Reprinted by permission of Roth Publishing Inc.

"Boy or Girl?" from *Collected Verse of Edgar A. Guest*. Copyright © 1934 by Contemporary Books, Inc. Reprinted by permission of the publisher.

"Boyhood" by Washington Allston from *The World's Best Poetry*, volume I, Home/Friendship, edited by Bliss Carman. Copyright © 1981 by Granger Book Co., Inc. Reprinted by permission of Roth Publishing Inc.

"Candida, for John Betjeman's Daughter" by Patrick Kavanagh from *Collected Poems* by Patrick Kavanagh. Copyright © 1964 by Patrick Kavanagh. Copyright © 1968, 1972 by Katherine B. Kavanagh. Reprinted by permission of Devin-Adair Publishers, Inc., Greenwich, CT 06830.

"Ceiling Zero" by Margaret Fishback from *Look Who's a Mother!* Copyright © 1945 by Margaret Fishback. Copyright renewed © 1972 by Margaret Fishback. Reprinted by permission of Simon & Schuster, Inc.

"Children" by Walter Savage Landor from *The World's Best Poetry*, volume I, Home/Friendship, edited by Bliss Carman. Copyright © 1981 by Granger Book Co., Inc. Reprinted by permission of Roth Publishing Inc.

"The Children" by Constance Urdang from *The Contemporary American Poets*. Reprinted by permission of the author.

"The Children and Sir Nameless" by Thomas Hardy reprinted with permission of Macmillan Publishing Company from *The Complete Poems of Thomas Hardy*, edited by James Gibson (New York: Macmillan, 1978).

146

INDEX OF TITLES

151

INDEX OF AUTHORS AND TRANSLATORS